Glow-in-the-Dark ZOMBIE SCIENCE

Glow-in-the-Dark ZOMBIE SCIENCE

TABLE OF CONTENTS

ZOMBIES 101	4
REAL-LIFE ZOMBIE ENCOUNTERS	5
WHAT CAUSES A ZOMBIE?	6
ZOMBIE LAB EXPERIMENT #1	8
WHAT DO ZOMBIES WANT?	10
ZOMBIE LAB EXPERIMENT #2	12
WHY DO ZOMBIES MOVE SLOWLY?	14
SLIME TIME!	16
DO ZOMBIES EVER SWIM?	18
ZOMBIE LAB EXPERIMENT #3	20
DO ZOMBIES TRAVEL IN GROUPS?	22
CAN ZOMBIES BE KILLED?	26
ZOMBIE LAB EXPERIMENT #4	28
ESCAPE A ZOMBIE	30
ZOMBIE KITCHEN	32

tangerine Press
an imprint of
Scholastic
www.scholastic.com

Copyright © 2009 Scholastic Inc.
Scholastic and Tangerine Press and associated logos are trademarks of Scholastic Inc.
Published by Tangerine Press, an imprint of Scholastic Inc., 557 Broadway, New York, NY 10012
10 9 8 7 6 5 4 3 2 1
ISBN: 978-0-545-22626-4
Printed and bound in Taipei, Taiwan

WHAT COMES IN YOUR KIT?

STICKY BRAIN
How cool is this: Your very own zombie brain! Now you know what to look for when you have to get rid of zombies. (See P. 29 for more ideas on what to do with your zombie brain.)

GLOW-IN-THE-DARK GROW ZOMBIE
Grow your own zombie without a virus. Put your grow zombie in a tub of water. The bigger the container, the bigger the zombie will grow. Once it's done growing, take it out and it will shrink back close to its original size. Then, you can grow it again. (See P. 19 for more zombie-growing fun.)

GLOW-IN-THE-DARK SLIME
To make the slime that came with your kit, pour the slime powder into your beaker. Add 2 tablespoons (30 ml) of water. Stir the water and slime mix until the powder dissolves. (See P. 17 for more slimy fun.)

GLOW-IN-THE-DARK DIAPER DUST
Put a large tablespoonful of diaper dust into a plastic baggie. Little by little, add water to the bag. Every time you add more water, squeeze the bag to mix the stuff. Keep adding water. You'll be amazed at how much you can add. Stop adding water when you feel like the squish is perfect. (See P. 25 for more Diaper Dust drama.)

BEAKER
Use your beaker to mix the slime.

WOODEN STIR STICK
Use the wooden stir stick to mix the slime powder.

ZOMBIES 101

TRUE OR FALSE?

- You're difficult to scare.
- You like to learn new things.
- You think zombies are pretty cool.

All true, of course! And these conclusions are based on one simple fact about you: You're reading this book.

There are simple facts and conclusions to be made about zombies! And here is the most important one of all:

ZOMBIES ARE REAL.

(Or at least let's assume that's a fact for the purposes of this book, okay?)

So, if zombies are real, what do you need to know about them? How about...um, everything!

For starters, zombies are incredibly powerful beings. If one were to walk right into your room in search of its next meal, **YOU** (unlike **IT**) would be practically powerless. That's because you're alive, you feel pain, and you're not all that scary. Not to mention, you wouldn't have a clue what to do during a zombie encounter!

How can you become more powerful in case such an unlikely (but entirely possible) event were to occur? First, even the smartest zombie experts will tell you that you should know your stuff. After all, information is power! Fortunately, everything you need to know in order to protect yourself during a zombie encounter awaits you between the covers of this book.

REAL-LIFE ZOMBIE ENCOUNTERS

Recorded zombie attacks date back to 60,000 B.C. in Central Africa. But the new millennium has seen its fair share of encounters. People the world over have reported zombie sightings—in Egypt, China, Scotland, Germany, Jerusalem, South America, Mexico, Brazil, the Soviet Union, and the United States in Oregon, Louisiana, and California, as well as many other places around the globe. Here are five particularly compelling stories:

- In the mid-1890s, professor and Egyptologist Sir William Matthew Flinders Petrie discovered dozens of headless corpses during his excavations—which archaeologists later suggested might have belonged to former zombies, based on the cut marks.

- In 1892, a British excavation team left an Egyptian tomb certain they had just discovered the burial ground of a zombie. The corpse's brain tested positive for a possible zombie-making virus—and the tomb's interior was covered with thousands of scratch marks. (It appeared that its "dead" resident had actually tried to claw its way out!)

- Famous author Zora Neale Hurston visited Haiti in 1937 with the specific purpose of investigating reports of zombies. While there, she claimed to have caught on film the first zombie ever photographed.

- While fishing in a California bay in 1994, three men say they "caught" a partially decomposed man who was still alive and who tried to attack them—even attempting to bite the neck of one of the men.

- In 2001, a Moroccan fishing village underwent mass hysteria when an unexplained neurological condition caused five villagers to try to attack their own friends and family members—all in the interest of eating them!

WHAT CAUSES A ZOMBIE?

Different cultures have different explanations for what causes a zombie. In Africa, people claim that Voodoo rituals can be used to "zombify" normal people. But some of today's scientists offer another theory: People become zombies because of a virus. Zombie expert Max Brooks has even given the "zombie virus" a name: "Solanum."

TINY TERRORS

Viruses are tiny "agents" that infect things. They are so tiny they can only be seen through microscopes. Viruses cause many different illnesses and diseases. Your body has probably battled at least a handful of viruses—most of which were probably colds or the flu.

For such a small thing, a virus packs quite a punch. In fact, a virus can make a person feel terribly sick—sometimes even sending him or her to bed for weeks!

In the case of the flu, a virus hitches a ride from one victim to another atop a droplet produced by a sneeze or cough. Flu viruses enter through the lungs, nose, or throat. Once inside, they reproduce billions of times and spread to more and more cells.

VIRUS BUSTERS

Protect yourself from viral infections by following these simple rules:

1. Wash your hands thoroughly with soap and/or an alcohol-based sanitizer.

2. Only touch your mouth, nose, and eyes when necessary and with clean hands.

3. Cover your mouth with a tissue when coughing or sneezing.

4. If you don't have a tissue, cough into your arm instead of your hand.

5. Stay away from other people with viruses whenever possible!

According to zombie-ologist Max Brooks, solanum (the "zombie virus") is spread through body fluids. Brooks claims most people become zombies when they are **bitten by zombies** but can also catch the virus through open wounds.

ZOMBIE LAB EXPERIMENT #1

Pass It On

Would you believe that less than 70 percent of Americans actually wash their hands after using the restroom? See for yourself the difference between hands that have been thoroughly washed and those that haven't by following the simple instructions below. And then pass on your discovery—instead of germs—to your friends!

YOU WILL NEED:

- Newspaper
- Friend or family member
- Apron or smock
- Timer
- Sink
- Blindfold
- Washable paint
- Soap
- Between five and 10 paper towels
- Paper

WHAT YOU DO

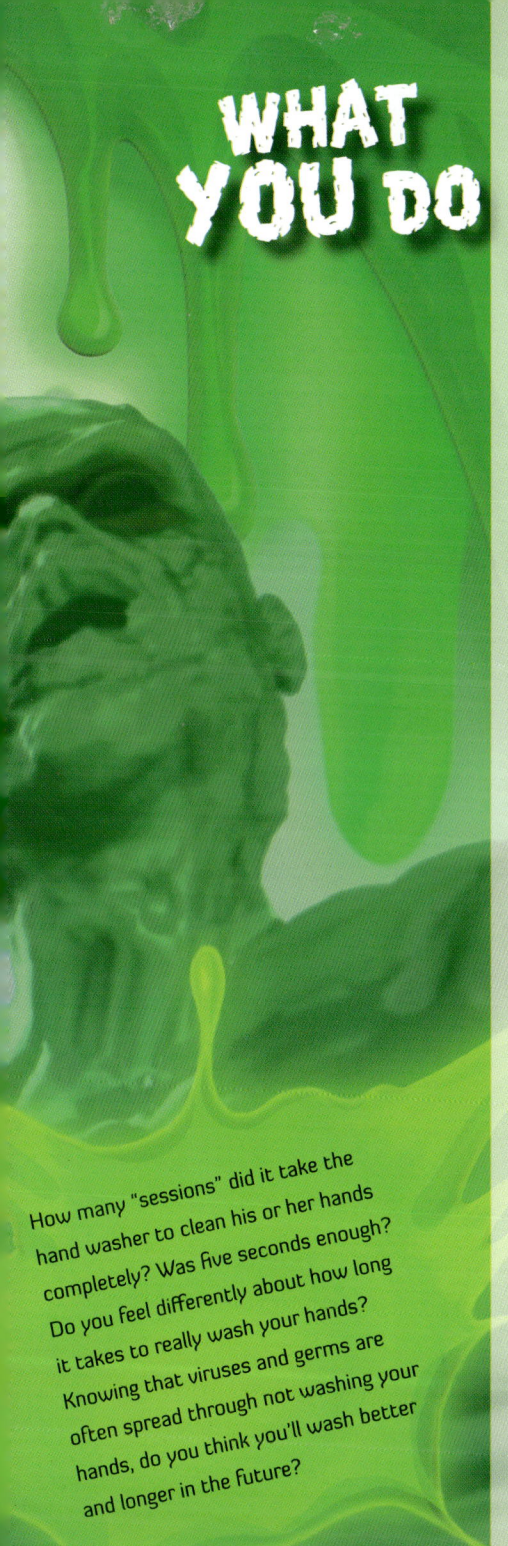

1. Cover a table or counter with newspaper.

2. One person (the hand washer) wears an apron or smock. The other person (the timekeeper) is in charge of the timer.

3. The timekeeper squeezes or spoons one teaspoon of the washable paint into the palm of the hand washer's hand.

4. The hand washer then spreads the paint evenly over both hands (including the backs and around the fingernails). Both wait for the paint to dry completely.

5. At the sink, the timekeeper puts the blindfold over the eyes of the hand washer.

6. The hand washer washes his or her hands with soap for just one second. Then, the timekeeper assists the hand washer in blotting his or her hands on a paper towel.

7. The hand washer then washes his or her hands at different intervals (for four more seconds, then five more, then six more, and so on), blotting after each session.

How many "sessions" did it take the hand washer to clean his or her hands completely? Was five seconds enough? Do you feel differently about how long it takes to really wash your hands? Knowing that viruses and germs are often spread through not washing your hands, do you think you'll wash better and longer in the future?

WHAT DO ZOMBIES WANT?

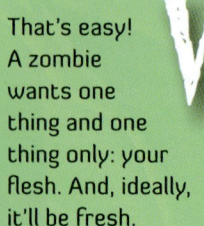

That's easy! A zombie wants one thing and one thing only: your flesh. And, ideally, it'll be fresh.

To understand where the zombie is coming from, think of yourself like a pizza. You're tastiest right now, when you're still warm. By tomorrow, you'll be a little more like a slice that was forgotten on a kitchen counter. And by next week, you'd be hard as a rock. So, when a zombie gets fresh meat, he really goes to town.

Sticking with the pizza analogy, you know when you've eaten one too many slices? Zombies don't get that feeling. That may sound good—but it's actually not. Because without his brain telling him when to quit, a zombie will continue to eat until he explodes. (Yuck!)

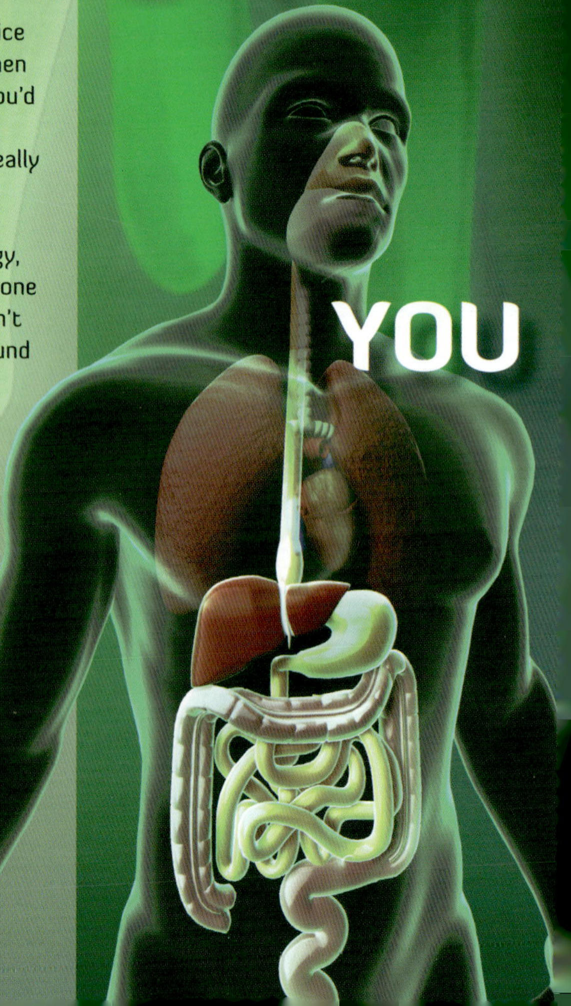

YOU

GOTTA GO!

The reason a zombie explodes when he has eaten too much is simple: he can't digest food. Try as he might, he simply won't get any nutrition out of a fruit salad or high-fiber cereal. (And he definitely won't see it later on in the bathroom for round two—because zombies aren't able to "go," either!)

The good news for you is that your system operates just fine. Here's what's going on in your digestive system (as opposed to a zombie's).

ZOMBIE

1. As you chew each bite, your mouth produces saliva. The saliva contains an enzyme that works to begin breaking down particles in the food.

2. The food moves through your esophagus and into your stomach, where digestive juices join the mix. Strong acids break apart proteins, sugars, and fats—making them easier for your body to manage.

3. The muscle at the end of your stomach relaxes. Now the food can move into your duodenum.

4. Inside your duodenum are more enzymes. They set to work, breaking down your food into even smaller particles.

5. Your body won't digest everything. Undigested waste (mostly roughage and water, in the form of a liquid) moves into your colon. As the waste passes through your colon on its way to your rectum, the water is absorbed.

6. The small, remaining portion of the waste waits inside your rectum—before being sent through your anus on its (dare we say merry?) way!

11

ZOMBIE LAB EXPERIMENT #2

In a Spit Second

Place a saltine cracker on your tongue. But resist the urge to chew and swallow it! Does it seem as if your mouth is kind of eating the cracker without you even chewing? Is it dissolving on your tongue? Why might that be happening? (Take a guess based on everything you just learned about the digestion process. For the answer, turn this page upside-down.)

ANSWER: The powerful chemicals and enzymes in your saliva will sometimes set to work even before you start chewing.

STOM-ICK STUFF

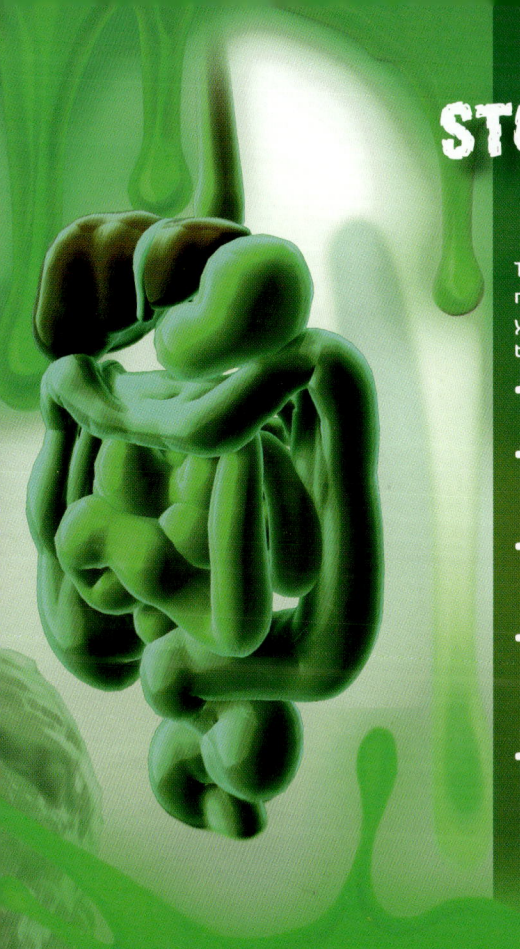

Think zombies are more shocking than normal people? These five facts about your digestive system will make you think again!

- Your stomach acid is strong enough to dissolve a piece of metal!
- Some foods can take more than three days for your stomach to process!
- A single fart contains five types of gas: nitrogen, oxygen, carbon dioxide, hydrogen, and methane!
- Technically, a person can digest food even when upside-down (with food being pushed "up" into his or her stomach)!
- A human stomach contains roughly 35 million digestive glands!

Extra Credit: If a zombie were to place a saltine cracker on his tongue, what do you think would happen?

Answer: If you guessed nothing, you'd be right! The enzymes necessary to break down the cracker are part of a working digestive system—which a zombie doesn't have.

WHY DO ZOMBIES MOVE SLOWLY?

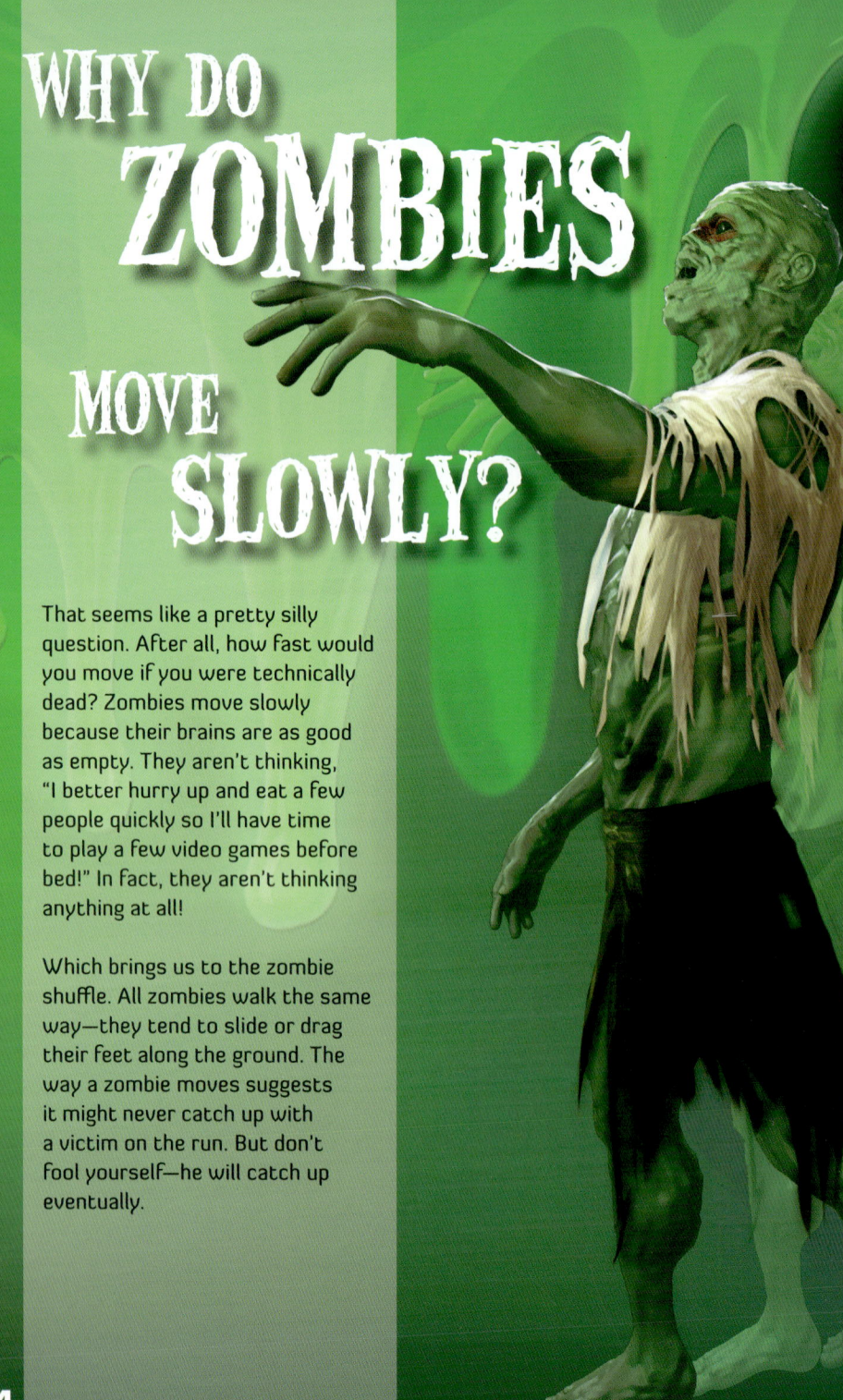

That seems like a pretty silly question. After all, how fast would you move if you were technically dead? Zombies move slowly because their brains are as good as empty. They aren't thinking, "I better hurry up and eat a few people quickly so I'll have time to play a few video games before bed!" In fact, they aren't thinking anything at all!

Which brings us to the zombie shuffle. All zombies walk the same way—they tend to slide or drag their feet along the ground. The way a zombie moves suggests it might never catch up with a victim on the run. But don't fool yourself—he will catch up eventually.

Some animals move much more quickly than others. A zombie wouldn't stand a chance against one of these 10!

SPEED DEMONS

Peregrine falcon	200 mph (321 kph)
Cheetah	70 mph (113 kph)
Pronghorn antelope	
Lion	40 mph (69 kph)
Thomson's gazelle	
Wildebeest	
Quarter horse	
Cape Hunting Dog	
Elk	
Coyote	

SLOW POKES

Garden Snail	.03 mph (.05 kph)
Three-toed sloth	
Giant tortoise	
Spider	
House mouse	8 mph (13 kph)
Chicken	12 mph (19 kph)
Pig	
Squirrel	
Black mamba snake	
Elephant	

SLIME TIME!

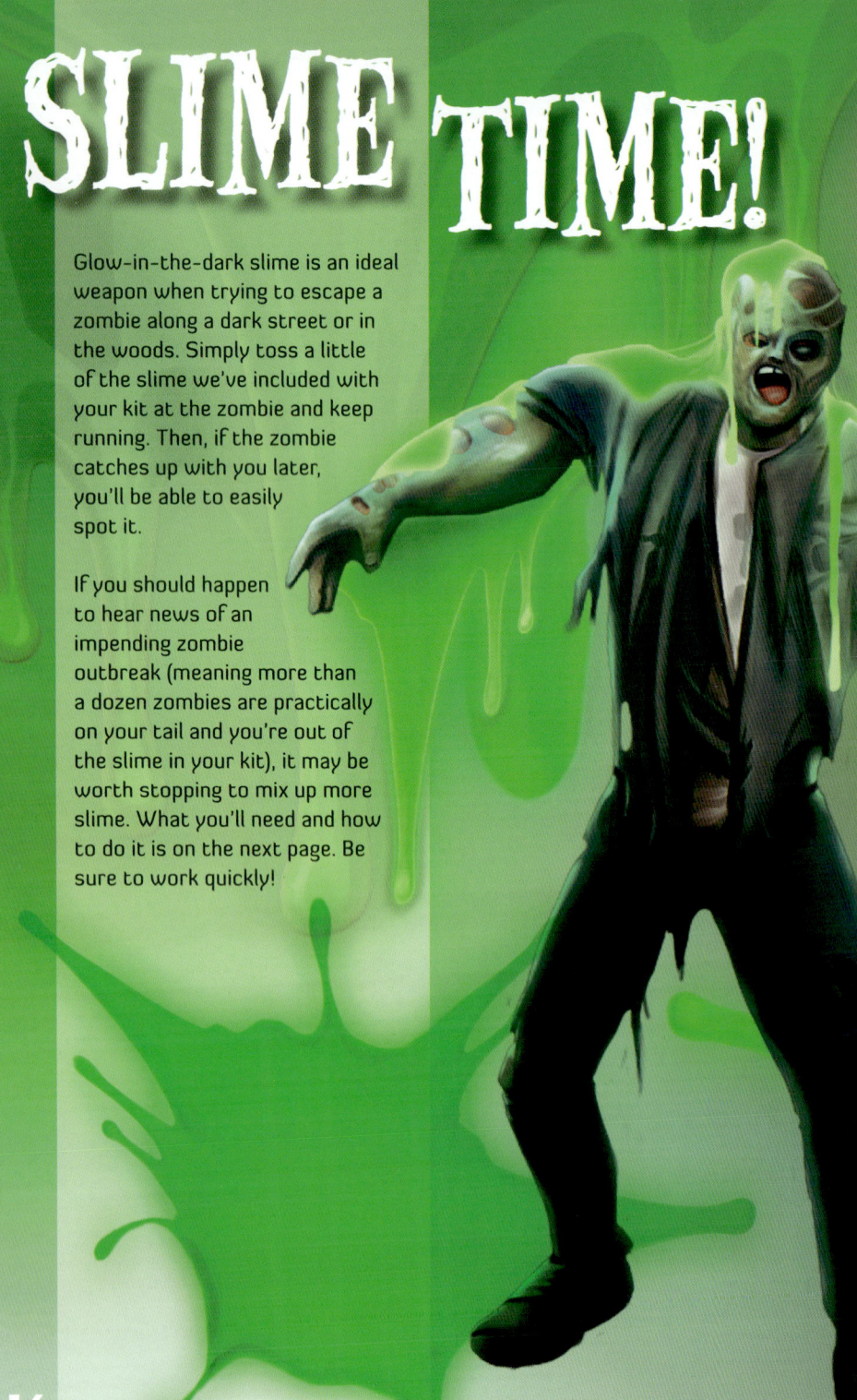

Glow-in-the-dark slime is an ideal weapon when trying to escape a zombie along a dark street or in the woods. Simply toss a little of the slime we've included with your kit at the zombie and keep running. Then, if the zombie catches up with you later, you'll be able to easily spot it.

If you should happen to hear news of an impending zombie outbreak (meaning more than a dozen zombies are practically on your tail and you're out of the slime in your kit), it may be worth stopping to mix up more slime. What you'll need and how to do it is on the next page. Be sure to work quickly!

MAKE MORE SLIME!

Oh no! You've run out of slime and there is a zombie attack? Quick, whip up this slime!

This slime is the perfect weapon against zombies, but it's not good for you. No tasting or eating the slime. Be sure to wash your hands when you're done with it.

And don't leave it anywhere that it might stain a surface in your home or anywhere else for that matter!

YOU WILL NEED:

- 2 cups (475 ml) of water
- A medium saucepan
- ½ cup (120 ml) cornstarch
- Glow-in-the-dark paint (found in craft stores)
- An adult helper

WHAT YOU DO

1. Pour the water into the saucepan.
2. The adult helper part starts here: Bring the water to a boil.
3. Add the cornstarch and stir.
4. Add 1 teaspoon (5 ml) of the paint, and stir constantly.
5. Remove the pan from the heat, and let the liquid cool to room temperature. The adult helper part ends here.
6. Wait until it has goo-ified enough for your zombie-marking pleasure!
7. Store your glow-in-the-dark slime in a resealable plastic bag or airtight container.

DO ZOMBIES EVER SWIM?

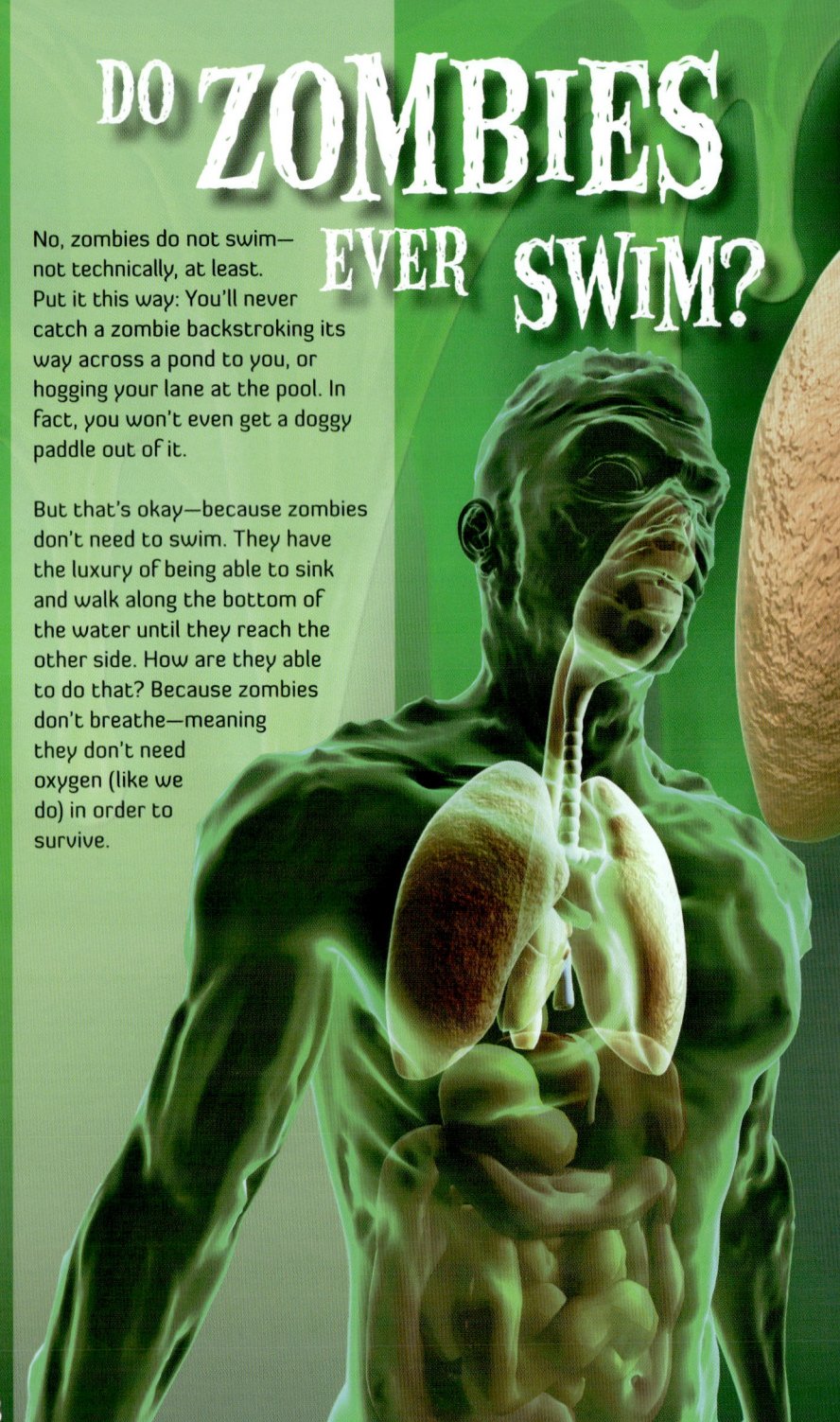

No, zombies do not swim—not technically, at least. Put it this way: You'll never catch a zombie backstroking its way across a pond to you, or hogging your lane at the pool. In fact, you won't even get a doggy paddle out of it.

But that's okay—because zombies don't need to swim. They have the luxury of being able to sink and walk along the bottom of the water until they reach the other side. How are they able to do that? Because zombies don't breathe—meaning they don't need oxygen (like we do) in order to survive.

INS AND OUTS

Unlike zombies, the cells in your body require oxygen. The air you breathe in keeps you alive.

When you inhale, you bring air into your nasal passages, which is filtered, moistened, and warmed.

The air moves past your windpipe, your vocal cords, and finally into your chest. Inside your chest, your windpipe splits into two tubes, each leading to one of your lungs.

Tiny sacs in your lungs escort the new oxygen from the air you breathed into your bloodstream.

Your red blood cells change from purple to a deep red as they receive the new oxygen, trading it for carbon dioxide that your body doesn't need. The carbon dioxide heads back up through your windpipe and exits when you exhale.

GROW ZOMBIE

So, you've grown your zombie. Now what? Here are a few things you can do with your grow guy!

- Keep it in a jar on your desk.
- Show off your pet zombie to your friends and family.
- See how many times you can grow it.

DID YOU KNOW...

- Your lungs are home to about 1,500 mi. (2,414 km) of airways.
- Plants take in the carbon dioxide we don't want—and give us oxygen in return.
- Young people require more oxygen than older people.

ZOMBIE LAB EXPERIMENT #3

Bad Breath Bandits

Billions of bacteria live in your mouth—on your tongue, between your teeth, and even in the back of your throat. Under the right circumstances (such as when you drink sports drinks or eat dairy products), the bacteria in your mouth grows quickly.

While bacteria grows, it also creates waste, which creates your bad breath. That is sometimes even nastier than a zombie smell!

When you eat foods that are high in proteins, the bacteria in your mouth produce waste that is sulfurous (which smells kind of like rotten eggs). So each time you eat a burger, the bacteria in your mouth make their own little meal out of it—and then produce some of that yucky-smelling waste. (The same goes for that filet of fish sandwich. And that yummy frozen yogurt, too!)

Find an honest friend to help you with the following experiment over the course of a few days. Sample as many of these foods as possible, in bite-size portions. (Just because you're going to wind up smelling like a zombie doesn't mean you need to eat like one!) Then make a chart and have your friend rate your breath about an hour after you've eaten each of these foods. Use a rating scale 1 to 5 with 5 being the worst. Which caused you to get a 5+?

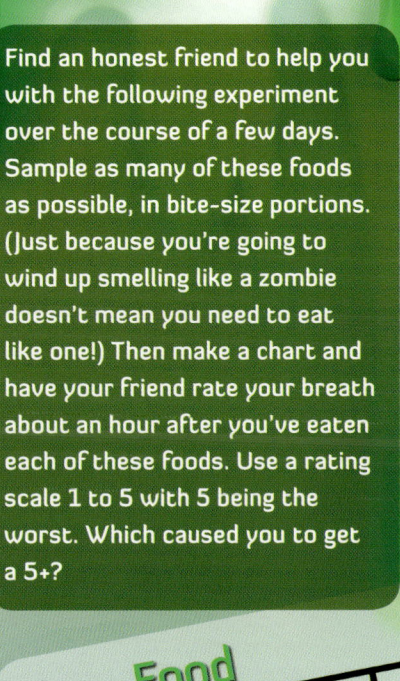

Food

- Tuna salad
- Slice of bacon
- Fried egg
- String cheese
- Large cup of milk
- Several forkfuls of beans
- Hunk of peanut butter
- Handful of sunflower seeds
- Cup of chicken soup
- Tofu cubes
- Yogurt-covered raisins

Rating

DO ZOMBIES TRAVEL IN GROUPS?

No sleepover is complete without a zombie-themed horror movie. So, it's safe to assume you've seen at least a handful of zombie flicks, right?

But do zombies travel in large masses? Actually, they don't! They don't benefit in any way whatsoever from group travel? Not really. But it is true that seeing 20 zombies is certainly scarier than one—which might be a benefit if you look at it through the scare-factor lens.

When zombies come together, it's actually more of a coincidence. They sense the same victims and move in the same direction. (It's definitely not as if one sent out a group text message saying: "Hey, let's all meet and go make mincemeat out of that little girl across the street!")

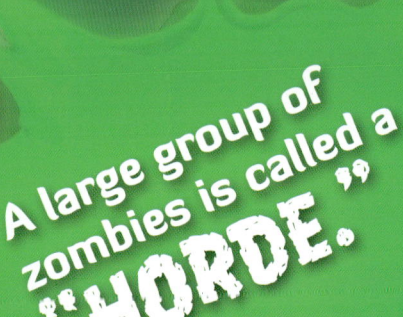

A large group of zombies is called a "HORDE."

Many animals travel in groups. Some groups of animals have names that are probably familiar to you. Below is a list of 30 animal names and their group names. Draw a line from the name to the correct group name.

Ants	Bed
Donkeys	Pride
Alligators	Intrusion
Oysters	Family
Jellyfish	Clan
Frogs	Army
Hyenas	Troop
Cheetahs	Pod
Mice	Mob
Beavers	Bask
Birds	Nursery
Geese	Swarm
Horses	Colony
Gerbils	Pit
Cockroaches	Lodge
Otters	Herd
Kangaroos	School
Raccoons	Brood
Wolves	Gaggle
Owls	Prickle
Spiders	Coalition
Whales	Bundle
Porcupines	Pack
Lions	Slew
Fish	Band
Sharks	Warren
Squirrels	Horde
Bees	Flock
Monkeys	Parliament
Rabbits	Squad

23

POWER IN NUMBERS

Many animals work, eat, and even sleep together. (Fortunately for us, zombies aren't smart enough to figure out just how dangerous they could be if they joined forces!)

- Ants divide their responsibilities between three classes or "castes": workers, queens, and males.
- Buffalo "vote" with their eyes on the direction in which they will move.
- Baboons sleep in cozy groups of up to 50.
- When a bat is sick, its friends and family will bring food back to it.
- A capuchin monkey won't share with a stranger—but it will with friends and family members!
- Elephants call to each other in sounds so low that humans can't hear them.
- A single fish separated from its school will immediately search for a new group to live with.
- Some honeybees dance atop their hives in order to communicate with the other bees in the hive.
- Squirrel monkeys live in groups of up to 500 members broken down into smaller "troops."
- A herd of zebra will scatter when running from a predator, resulting in a confusing mass of vertical lines.

THE ULTIMATE WEAPON
ZOMBIE POWDER

Here are some ways to use your new glow-in-the-dark zombie powder (better known as diaper dust) in case of a zombie attack. Mix up a batch following the instructions on P. 3.

- Leave a trail of zombie powder mix behind you (like bread crumbs). A zombie will follow your trail thinking it's your flesh. Then, you can head off in another direction. It's the perfect escape.

- Attach the zombie powder to the outside of your backpack. If a zombie is following you, drop the zombie powder on the sidewalk and add water—instant slippery stuff to throw the zombie off your trail.

- Keep the mixed-up zombie powder in a plastic baggie. It's the perfect way to signal friends and family while you're on the run.

CAN ZOMBIES BE KILLED?

Killing a zombie is about as difficult as getting a 100 on a math test. It's nearly impossible to kill a zombie—since none of its systems work anyway! (As you may know, a zombie doesn't feel pain. It doesn't have blood. And it doesn't need air.)

Zombies are like cockroaches—they can survive practically anything. Luckily, there is one way to kill a zombie, but it's by no means easy: REMOVE ITS BRAIN! There is a sticky zombie brain in your kit, so you know what to look for!

LIFE WITHOUT YOUR BRAIN WOULD BE TOTALLY IMPOSSIBLE!

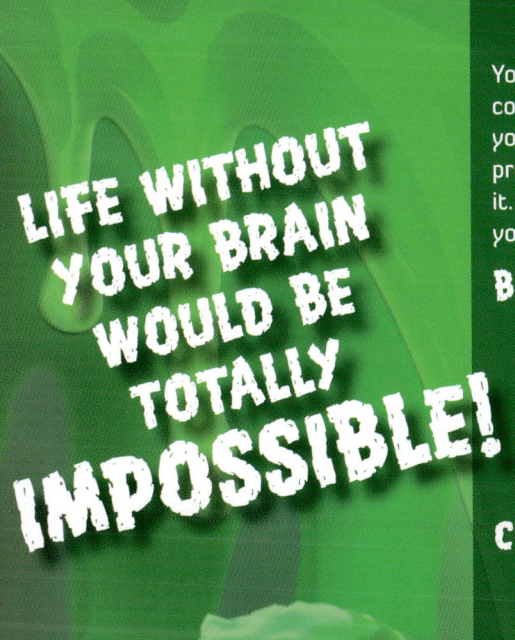

Your brain rules your body, controlling almost everything you do—which means you should probably know a little more about it. You can begin by familiarizing yourself with its five main parts:

BRAIN STEM:
Your brain stem connects your brain and spinal cord. It oversees everything you need to live, including your breath and blood flow.

CEREBRUM:
This is the heaviest part of your brain. When you want your body to do something (such as hop on one foot or tap a piano key), your cerebrum gives your muscles their marching orders.

CEREBELLUM:
The cerebellum is at the back of your brain. It is in charge of coordinating your balance and coordination.

HYPOTHALAMUS:
Your hypothalamus acts like a thermostat. It tells your body to sweat when it's hot and to shiver when you're cold.

PITUITARY GLAND:
This part of your brain is the size of a pea. It regulates your growth and controls how much sugar and water are in your body.

DID YOU KNOW?
On average, a human brain thinks about 70,000 thoughts in a day.

ZOMBIE LAB EXPERIMENT #4

I Scream, You Scream...

We all scream for ice cream!

Anyone who has eaten too much ice cream too quickly knows what "brain freeze" feels like—and it's terrible. Brain freeze happens when something very cold touches your mouth's palate (the smooth area on the roof of your mouth). While the nerves around your palate send messages to your brain, your blood flow is altered. The result is pain.

Luckily, brain freeze isn't dangerous—and it doesn't last long!

Studies have proven that at least 30 percent of people get ice cream headaches. Gather 10 friends or family members for an ice cream party—but don't share with them your purpose for the get-together. Ask each to eat a bowl of ice cream as quickly as possible. When everyone has finished, hand out a written questionnaire asking each if he or she suffered any sort of discomfort while eating the ice cream so quickly. If so, have them share the details about their experiences. Collect the responses and review your data. If at least three people responded that they experienced brain freeze, your study supports the outstanding research on this topic!

WHAT TO DO WITH A ZOMBIE BRAIN?

- Put it in a jar and show everyone your zombie brain.
- Add a little slime to a jar, and put the brain in the slime for added effect.
- Softly toss your slimy brain onto a window and watch it slide down. (You'll have to clean up those marks.)
- Use your slimy, sticky brain as a stress reliever. Squish it every time you get mad.
- Toss it at a zombie. It might like it better than yours!

DID YOU KNOW?
When you yawn, you actually help your brain to wake up.

WHAT ARE SOME OF THE BEST WAYS TO ESCAPE A ZOMBIE?

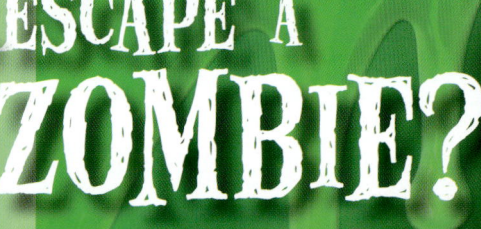

Max Brooks—the worldwide authority on all things zombie—claims that zombies cannot climb. With this in mind, what kinds of things can you climb up or on when escaping a zombie? How about climbing bridges, climbing jungle gyms (playgrounds have great ones!), hills, ladders, mountains, stairs, steps, and walls (low enough to climb).

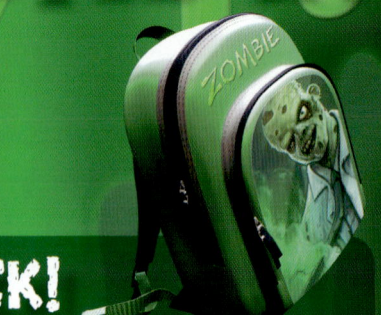

PACK FOR ATTACK!

You're good at packing your backpack. But have you ever packed a zombie escape bag? Here are some must-haves.

- Water bottle—after all, staying hydrated is part of staying alive!
- Some snack items—trail mix, granola bars, and canned foods are best.
- Flashlight—don't forget replacement batteries.
- Morse code chart—see below.
- Glow-in-the-dark slime—see P. 17.
- Glow-in-the-dark zombie powder (or diaper dust)—see P. 25.
- Sticky brain—see P. 29.
- Address book—know where your friends and family members live!
- Homework—it's unlikely you'll have time to study, but who knows?
- Cell phone—if you have one, definitely bring it.
- Foldable map—you need to know where you're going.
- Toothbrush and toothpaste—avoid zombie breath!
- Change of clothes—camouflage colors are ideal.
- Family picture—it can get lonely on the run.
- Notebook and pen or pencil—in case of the worst, you'll want people to know your story!

Flashlights can come in handy if you want to send silent messages through Morse code to friends, family members, or other potential victims. Invented in the 1840s by Samuel F. B. Morse, Morse code was developed to facilitate early radio communication. Morse code is often sent through sound—but it can also be sent through light. Copy this Morse code alphabet and bring it with you on the run.

Dots = short flashes. Bars = long flashes.

A	• ▬	N	▬ •	1	• ▬ ▬ ▬ ▬
B	▬ • • •	O	▬ ▬ ▬	2	• • ▬ ▬ ▬
C	▬ • ▬ •	P	• ▬ ▬ •	3	• • • ▬ ▬
D	▬ • •	Q	▬ ▬ • ▬	4	• • • • ▬
E	•	R	• ▬ •	5	• • • • •
F	• • ▬ •	S	• • •	6	▬ • • • •
G	▬ ▬ •	T	▬	7	▬ ▬ • • •
H	• • • •	U	• • ▬	8	▬ ▬ ▬ • •
I	• •	V	• • • ▬	9	▬ ▬ ▬ ▬ •
J	• ▬ ▬ ▬	W	• ▬ ▬	0	▬ ▬ ▬ ▬ ▬
K	▬ • ▬	X	▬ • • ▬		
L	• ▬ • •	Y	▬ • ▬ ▬		
M	▬ ▬	Z	▬ ▬ • •		

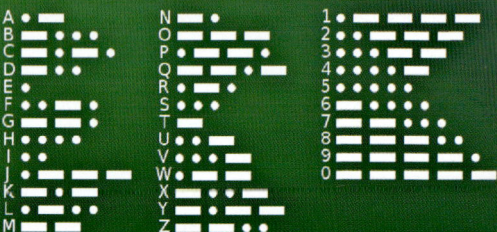

WHAT WOULD THEY EAT?

Severed Fingers
Makes about 4 dozen fingers!

YOU WILL NEED:

- 1 cup (237 ml) butter
- 1 cup (237 ml) sugar
- 1 egg
- 1 teaspoon (5 ml) vanilla extract
- 3 cups (720 ml) flour
- 1-1/2 teaspoons (7.5 ml) baking powder
- 1/2 teaspoon (2.5 ml) salt
- Large bowl
- Butter knife
- Clear and red decorator gel
- Almond slivers
- Baking sheet

Adult supervision is required! This recipe involves a knife and an oven!

Zombies don't cook. And they don't care about measurements. (They're definitely not wondering how many calories are in your thigh or how much protein they might get by eating your toes!)

1. Preheat your oven to 350°F (176°C).
2. Cream the butter and sugar by whipping them together in a bowl.
3. Stir in the eggs and vanilla.
4. Mix in the flour, baking powder, and salt.
5. Set the bowl in the fridge to chill for two hours.
6. Take a small handful of the dough and roll it into a long tube resembling a finger.
7. Line an ungreased baking sheet with your "fingers." Place the fingers 2 inches (5 cm) apart. Continue until the baking sheet is full.
8. Make indentations like knuckle lines in the middle of each finger with your butter knife. Also make indentations where you'll put the almond slivers (which will be the fingernails).
9. Bake them for 8 to 10 minutes (or until their edges begin to turn brown).
10. Let the "fingers" cool for 10 minutes.
11. One by one, fill each fingernail indentation with the clear decorator gel. Then, hold an almond sliver in place until the gel has dried and the nail is secure.
12. To make these "fingers" even more disgusting, squeeze red gel on them to look like blood.

31

ZOMBIE KITCHEN

The following zombie-friendly foods are so disgusting you might not want to even look at them, let alone eat them!

BOOGER STICKS:
Mix green food coloring with soft cheese and then dip pretzels into it!

BLOODY EYEBALLS:
Remove the yolks from hard-boiled eggs, press a large green olive into the center of each egg (pimiento side up), and then use a toothpick and red food coloring to give the eyes bloody vessels!

MOLDY PASTA:
Put some grated cheese in a resealable plastic bag, add a few drops of green food coloring, shake, and then sprinkle it over your pasta!

PIMPLE POPPERS:
Fill cored cherry tomatoes with cream cheese, and then give them a gentle squeeze!

HOW CAN I MAKE MYSELF LOOK LIKE A ZOMBIE IN THE KITCHEN?

- Shuffle around the kitchen
- Moan each time you handle a new ingredient
- Stagger between counters
- Dust your hair with flour
- Refuse to smile when people enter the room
- Stare ahead blankly in between courses
- Keep your eyes halfway closed (when not reading recipes)